Fo

'Som

a god is hiding. Can
you see him?'

Best

*Elsewhere or
Thereabouts*

Alasdair Paterson

*Elsewhere
or
Thereabouts*

Shearsman Books

First published in the United Kingdom in 2014 by
Shearsman Books
50 Westons Hill Drive
Emersons Green
BRISTOL
BS16 7DF

Shearsman Books Ltd Registered Office
30–31 St. James Place, Mangotsfield, Bristol BS16 9JB
(this address not for correspondence)

www.shearsman.com

ISBN 978-1-84861-327-0

Cover design by Alys Paterson.

ACKNOWLEDGEMENTS
Some of these poems, sometimes in earlier versions, appeared in the
following magazines: *The Broadsheet, Great Works; Like starlings; Molly
Bloom; Shadowtrain*; and in the following anthologies: *High on the Downs:
a festschrift for Harry Guest* (ed. Tony Lopez); *Newspaper Taxis: Poetry after
the Beatles* (ed. Phil Bowen, Damian Furniss and David Woolley);
Sea Pie: a Shearsman anthology of Oystercatcher Poetry (ed. Peter Hughes);
The Shuffle Anthology, 2010-2011.

in arcadia was published as a pamphlet by Oystercatcher Press in 2011.

Contents

Homerics

for Iain and Bob

For of great Homer, men say that he came from this country or that island, from such times as he sings of or less ancient days, that he was one man or many, and all of which may be to say, that he was no-one and all men, and so you, and so me.

Jonathan Hobday: *Mirabile visu: discoveries of roads and ruins*

Age of gold

Burnish the armour.
Drench the altar.
Flourish the treasure.

Or walk out
into a flare of sunlight
that's all that matters
here, this moment.

Those gods you named
and brought to life
seem to like you.
Days like this, you might
expect to hear from one.

Pellucid, bright
as a rock-pool at sunrise
is how oracles speak
the day before
the age of second thoughts

Age of migrations

Through the swirl
and settle of black beer
surge the night-crossings,
deep and sharp.
Out of the shore-mist
into jolts of dark
and you're cleared
all at once to begin
the long losing game,
remembering.

Remembering arteries
of fuchsia and rust,
stone penned by stone,
all roads the road away;
the music in your head
a smoky flute
hard at the songbook
of empty rooms.

Leaving:
that taste nothing drowns.
That drained glass.

Age of glossaries

wine-dark: contentious epithet for the sea, conjuring up an unlikely overlap of colour ranges, though a glorious sunset or volcanic ash in the atmosphere (see *Atlantis*) may indeed tint the marine landscape with red or purple. This locution seems to have nothing at all to do with battle-stains (see also *rosy-fingered*).

long-shadowed spear: sun, plain, the advance of the phalanx, shadows pushing in front to create an avant-garde. The travelling shadow of a spear thrown into the air. The degree of visibility of death's approach. The strike. Familiar discussions of the destined and the random.

blinded: here, not by blood or sweat but by an intervention of the gods, perhaps in the form of mist or that moment's fatigued distraction fatal in a battle with edged weapons. In these moments, a wounded enemy can be spirited away or your death-blow come at you unseen.

timeless bronze: now at the bottom end of war-gaming accoutrements, in its day the bronze breastplate was often glorious with sophisticated decoration and adequately resistant to bronze age weapons. Nothing at the sharp end of the arms race is however destined to be timeless. Nor its wearer.

clattered: a noisy impact, both transitive and intransitive: here, the soundtrack of falling metal carapaces encasing compromised flesh, the audible transition from animate to inanimate, the fall of puppets with their strings cut.

Olympians: soon enough, though, gods lose interest in competitive puppeteering, in the butcher's bill and the hecatombs of offerings, and head off for feasts and adventures elsewhere.

Probably they think their own time of reckoning will never come. It will come.

feasting: a definitive epic activity, enmeshed in societal expectations of largesse and obligation, a counterpoint to battlefield heroics and terrors. Uncomfortably, with the reference to dogs and birds, we are reminded that the battlefield is, for the rest of the natural world, the banquet.

darkness: see *surge of death.*

darkness: see *soul flits weeping.*

darkness: see *night enfolded him.*

Age of bards I

Years and years of it,
blind scrabbling on the heartstrings,
years choked with the suppressed,
undischarged, abandoned
but never gone, never gone,
till there was no room in me,
till in the end
what alternative had I,
nothing for it
but the old measures.

Every day now
I'm back in bard school.
I'm trying hard.
I must try harder.
I'm trying harder.

Familiar, the blacked-out room.
Familiar, the stone on the chest.
Familiar, descent. Ascent.
Then.

Age of oracles

To begin with, the question.

No, surely, first of all, the problem. Then the question. Like: The pre-emptive strike, yes or no? Peace through marriage: what are the chances? How much flex should there be in consanguinity taboos? Why has a certain goddess got it in for us and what/who should be sacrificed?

The problem, the question, the stifling multiplicity of solutions, the labyrinth of futures, the weary decision to consult the oracle.

The decision, the journey. The toll exacted by mountains, forests, seas. The bedraggled arrival at the sanctuary.

The arrival, the wash and brush-up, the priestly interview. The outline of the problem. The sacrifice, the payment. The audience with the oracle.

The audience with the oracle. The tripod above the smoking fissure in the rock. The rolling, drugged eyes, the babble. The priest primed from the interview to tidy up the utterance. The official response, cadenced and impenetrable.

The arduous return home with the response. The understanding or misunderstanding. The action. The success or the catastrophe. Whichever, full credit to the oracle.

Somewhere in there, the god is hiding. Can you see him?

Age of bronze

You gave the wounds.
You took the wounds.
Not all the wounds
were at the front.
Nevertheless.

You shared a sorceress' bed.
You wore out your welcome
with another sorceress.
The sorceresses were chalk and cheese.
Nevertheless.

You swore an oath.
You broke an oath.
Your words blew away
like spindrift.
Nevertheless.

Nevertheless
the wound you survive
is the scar you can live with;
sea-winds cancel spells,
salt spoils honeycomb;
and when it comes to
undertakings and offences
your memory is only
as short as anyone's.

Agreed.
Now and at last,
you're ready to go home.

Age of bards II

The continuing tradition of wandering blind bards is to be considered a provocation for the following reasons:
1) Their endless wanderings spread the bacilli of gossip, dissent and other poisons.
2) Their stock-in-trade stories, full of superstition and the deeds of heroes in a feudal setting, seduce the minds of the credulous and challenge correct Party narratives.
3) Consciously or inadvertently, they draw demeaning parallels between past conflicts and beliefs and those of the post-revolutionary present.
4) They have proved resistant to the normal programmes of re-education.
5) They are, in the final analysis, incapable of any existence but that of the wandering blind bard.

Action recommended:
1) Conference on the oral poetry of wandering blind bards.
2) Maximum attendance of wandering blind bards.
3) Transcription of bardic materials by approved folklorists for future study in a hygienic and ideologically orthodox environment.
4) Post-conference social programme including escorted tour of typical regional forest.
5) Disappearance of wandering blind bards.

Age of stone

The night wood
of broken columns.

Heroes the colourway
Death-Mask Moon
gone astray and crumbling.

The air already filched
their bright colours and
rubbed away their eyes.
The weight of small birds
is too much for them.

Loser's arithmetic
they always struggled with
but still that applies:
subtraction tending to the point
beyond, the less than nothing,
footprints sunk in a plinth
like a myth of escape,
a myth of punishment.

How much they saw once.
How sad they are
now the stars have lost
their singing voices.
How they wish the gods
would get well again.

How little they seem
to have learned, after all.

Age of fire

Don't let it bring you down.
It's not the smoke
from funeral pyres,
not crematorium deposit
on childhood games,
not another city burning,
not here, not tonight
though someone whispers
all fires are the fire.

It's not oil flares
at the refinery,
not a red dwarf
tracked from the observatory,
not the sfumato
of Last Judgements;
just another humdrum done
day rolled to the furnace
in best sunset pinks and blues,
just another deathbed conversion
to the *quattrocento*.

Then there's black space
and mouthfuls from our flask,
each one a five minutes' heartbeat;
all fires the stolen fire
I think, as we walk
under the lamps
towards our own blaze.

Age of similes

Like an old rocker who's wasted
all his line-ups and his comebacks
but can't let go, no way, and takes
some rackety journeymen and kids
back on the road to the Wild Wild East,
the Road To Ruin Tour, far from jibes
about The Elderly Brothers or Simply
Remaindered or The Dewdrop Explodes;
and weeks down the road, is found dead
in a hotel room in downtown Vladivostok,
czarina-sized bed stacked with empty
vodka bottles and the kind of young Russian
who knocks at your door in the small hours
wearing nothing but a bad fur coat,
when your only comment should be *I can't
talk to you now, I'm in my pyjamas…*

So wily Odysseus, tired of palaces
and tapestry and unopened horizons,
planned a last one-way adventure
and sent out the Ithacan press-gang…

So blind Homer rattled to his feet,
pushing dementia away like a man
who fends off a wild boar with a harp,
to launch *Odyssey II*, the final sequel…

So the ageing flâneur, surveying
life on his provincial boulevards
and finding in his coffee cup
a great ship and cliffs of landfall

or shipwreck, wondered again if ruin
was the journey out from Ithaca, safe
harbour and quietude, or the voyage
that took you back there...

So...

Age of bards III

The song is an epic. The song is a myth. The song is an allegory of sacrificial kings and priestesses. The song is a glorification of trade wars. The song is a palimpsest. The song is a consolidation. The song is in all the libraries. There are no more bards to sing the song.

Before, when there were bards, they met a commission of scholars. The scholars listened and wrote down variations and juggled manuscripts and carved the approved version of the song. What was contradictory and incoherent was swept away. This heroic death survived, others disappeared, as the song entered the libraries.

Before that, everyone who had known one dead man in the song died too. In inherited memory, in the song, the dead man became a great warrior. He grew a genealogy of kings and immortals. He fought in a long war the gods manipulated. He was the favourite of one god, the enemy of another. He died among the reeds with the river nymphs cradling him. He was killed by an spear like a thunderbolt, a sword in the shape of an autumn leaf, an arrow that bristled like a reed. The river he crawled to flowed red with blood/was choked with bodies/had been dried by divine anger. The spear or sword or arrow was guided by one god and not deflected by another. He loved a princess/a priestess/a warrior on his side/a warrior on the other side and he/she avenged him/died of grief/forgot him quickly.

Before that, after the war ended, the fighters went their separate ways. The bard who first made the song, with the dead man in it among so many dead, took to the road, led by his boy. He was in demand. Men who never knew the dead man or his friends heard the song and loved it and asked for it again. The bard died, but by then the boy and others knew his lines and the song reached men who had never heard the bard. The song reached other bards. And others. It grew.

Before that, the bard who made the song heard about the dead man from friends drinking to his memory. Perhaps they made sure of this. He tried to place a voice, a presence. He wasn't certain that he could. He liked the image of a death by the water though, among the reeds. The dead man entered the bard's song. In the song he killed his enemy and took his wound at the front. The water sang to him. A cloud came down.

Before all that, a man took his wound and crawled to the riverbank and died there. Friends, stained by the skirmish, found him. They wept and tried to wash him but were glad that, for today, they were still alive. They sang, solemnly enough. The water was cool and clear. They drank. Tentatively, they found the first words for him.

Age of wisdom

Keep your friends close
but your scapegoats closer.

***

The nearer your immortality,
the more desperate
your body double.

***

Your famous battlefields:
but tomorrow, just
seven more versions of pastoral?

***

What is the thunder saying?
It says: yes, still alive
but not, definitely not,
out of the woods yet.

***

All your subjects' best stories
should crackle with a fire.
Preferably one you lit yourself.

***

Fake coins on the eyelids:
a sign something has gone
amiss in the family.
Too late, though.

***

The angry ghost module:
for those outcomes
the soothsayers unaccountably
missed.

ELSEWHERE
OR
THEREABOUTS

...if one just keeps on walking, everything will be all right.
Søren Kierkegaard: *Autobiographical journals and papers*

The solitary walker is never alone.
Jacques Mercier: *Out without Rousseau*

Noctivagation to an air by John Martyn

All morning
I was humming that song
about the road to ruin.

After a late lunch
I got going.

Nightfall, torchlight:
what does it look like, ruin?

Walk beginning and ending
with lines by Harry Guest

In Sho's
wild garden irises and a persimmon-tree,
the skyline circled by dark green mountains.

Harry, the valley stores are out
of persimmon and most other things
apart from mutton pies and whisky
and value packs of caramel wafers.
Life expectancy, mysteriously, is surging;
they must be digging for longevity
out in the bungalow plots, under the hills,
between boggy meadows where irises
flourish under another language banner.

Here, up close, the mountain's green
is different every brushstroke, darkened
or lightened by the feud between
pine shadow and rhododendron smother.
I'm past the tree-line, breathing hard,
scuffing the geology at the top
and I'll concede it's harder now
each time I make the climb; I'll have
my work cut out to get back down
before night clatters through the trees.

So I'm hankering for that kind
of pavilion, not even a mansion,
you'll see in oriental painting;
you know the kind of thing, refuge
for poets and sages and painters

and starved souls needing nourishment.
Nothing much but a roof, a bed, a fire
and the verandah for wine-drinking,
for viewing the modulations of green
as the day sinks and moonlight
picks out rock faces and stray trees;
for letting the landscape inside to make
its own geology there, shifting and
abrading, a tug like long time passing;
for picking up the siren song of vertigo
we don't always want to listen to,
but have to hear and fill our pages with.

And after a quiet night, the dawn up
early and scrambling to the valley, there
at the intersection of *solitary* and *lonely*
I'd remember what life I have down there
and how little I can be without my
dearest people; and, yesterday logged
in notebooks and muscles, pack
everything I need to take away.

And starting down among the trees
I might not see again, I'd watch them
ease themselves from the chilly quilt
of darkness, sway gently through
their morning exercises to a broadcast
of bird music that the light fine-tunes,
Harry, that sweetens for another
breath, another day, *this cage of air.*

Dander Round the Loch
with Henry Raeburn and James Hutton

Disconcerting,
the back of my hand
once the winter sun's out.
I can make out
mourning crepe,
an old rubbed hymnal,
a skinny craquelure
something like ice.
Mother, I think
it's come at last:
my skating minister vocation.

But can it be done
again, insouciant glide
in muffler and red laces?
Our ice is getting thinner
and frost by now
has powdered many
a Marie Antoinette.
Don't look, your reverence,
behind you—the rock
spat out and cooled,
biding its time,
inquiring hammers resonating
there, now and indefinitely
on *no vestige of a beginning*
on *no prospect of an end.*

Near-stasis
in the style of Ingmar Bergman

Old bones, old stalker,
we know that was you
came close to the windows last night
to leave a shrivelled bough,
a shrivelled bird.

We understand:
it's what you do.
We won't take it amiss.
After all we're quite the philosophers
here, six Buddhas in a row:
the standard shaven heads
and the factory seam
straight down the middle.

All we're saying is
please take as a token
these signed x-rays,
not our best likenesses
but (so far) our truest.
Which only means
stalk discreetly for now
and someday probably
we won't mind making friends.

Meantime we're practising
the stare that's not for visitors.
You know the one: that goes beyond
beds and windows, boughs and birds
and stars, and all we know there is.

Coastal path
around some lines by Lee Harwood

A thought came to me back there:
how Alpine the seaside is, white crests
that sweep in like fast-forward geology,
gardens abseiling down the cliffs in slo-mo.
Then the thought whistled off towards
oompah bands and paramilitary youth camp,
so I waved it goodbye and took the cliff path.

Gulls shriek in the air above the rock
while below thrift and small orchids flower
in that awesome hush between the waves breaking

And this is where I am now, Lee.
It's that salty dog breath hits me up here
and I shouldn't look down. I look down.
A hush, another skirmish; every day
and night the sea's at the white cliff
taking back its dead, but there's no hurry.

It's where I come once in a while
to listen to my disappeared, knowing
they're never short of a word or two.
I'd say they like it here, so far above
the dim, cold strand, beyond amours
and griefs strung out along the phone lines.

There's no hurry; they'll stay as long as I sit,
one hand clutching grass, my life in the other.
I look down. They say: your life, you'll
remember how heavy it is. How light.

Nostalgia trip,
words and music by Leonard Cohen

They opened the door of the big gaunt house
near the river, the Sisters of Mersey, at home
where you'd hear fog-horns on New Year's Eve,
where you'd float in the tree-tops on smoke and
patchouli.
And the shine of puzzle-rings and hardly dented
laughter
cheered all the ghosts of the housemaid attic
that cats teetered up to on Jacob's ladders
of lashed planks, Byzantine souls soaring
from spectral rosebeds, fallen robins, middle-earth.

Sister style was market stall and jumble sale,
a willed dishevelment, and though I was never
quite on that wavelength, Leonard sang
while they fed me tea and oranges a long time out
of China, the milk a little broken and the fruit
a fife-and-drum parade, orange blooming true-blue.

Now I don't keep track of each scattered Sister,
moved to elsewhere or thereabouts, though one's
treated me to a life-share on a long-loan basis.
The big house by the river, that's gone the way
of all the cats and all their kittens, but fog-horns
still mourn across the Mersey and Leonard came
on TV last night, new tunes about old skin
(down a tone or two). It's good we're all still here.
It's good I don't wake at twilight any more
to wonder who I am and sorrow at the answers.
That's all. I don't play his songs that often.

THE LIVERPUDLIAD

for Malone

Liverpool I love your horny-handed tons of soil.
Adrian Henri: *Liverpool poems*

pier head

this was always
a good place
to get your heart broken
and find a song
to patch it
I don't say mend

last ferry last train
or under the salty
tons of mersey
in radio silence
neon on the windscreen
just sing will you and
find someone to tell you
worse things happen at sea

they did too out there
beyond the emigration piers
beyond the slavery piazzas
the lightening cargoes
pitching westwards
the musics nursed barely
alive for a new soil

where they scattered and flowered
and seeded and mingled
and came back here on
vinyl under seamen's arms
so off we went again
stratocaster and hofner
jangling and thumping
new songs for old
for new heartbreaks

just sing will you
just sing

worse things happen

§

the grapes

the sozzled singalong years
ah there were giants
on the earth those days
and they had their seasons
like the famous albie
widger in apple-blossom time

the fireplace was notoriously
haunted and someone in the grate
somewhere heard every word
while the continents drifted
audibly as you sang
see the pyrenees along the nile

then it was our moment
the young ones who were
loosening the sky with diamonds
to a burglar sound of broken
glass till there was light
we'd been forbidden

I remember it well
that translucence
the beautiful liquids
it was the dawning
of the age of aquariums

shaw street

it tested our repertoire
and patience
that residency at the red
star social club

every time I picked
up the mandolin
someone wanted advice
on tuning his balalaika
and the drunk always woke
at some point to shout
comrades do you
know guantanamera

when we'd already
established all we knew
was the two word refrain
and the creepy spoken bit
from the sandpipers'
version that went
the words mean
I am a truthful man
from the land of
the palm trees

but we weren't unkind
we gave him a quick chorus
then lulled him back to sleep
with some flaming verses
from working class hero

now that
was something to be

sefton park

the opium eating episode
might have been a mistake

the bench we sat on
blazed wavering woodgrain
and as the landscape
twitched its skin
like an abyssinian cat
dreaming of flamingos
joni with her dulcimer
walked out of the lake
strumming and singing
oh I could drink
a case of honey dew

we opened the doors
of the palmhouse
that had floated down
from a medieval paradise
just in time to witness
the ascent to heaven
of the douanier rousseau
impresario of tropical rain forests
up a pure white spiral stair
beret on the slant
palette dripping
lily and geranium
and then I really needed
that sofa preferably
without the wild beasts
but we made it home

twenty-odd years later
in another glasshouse
I was considering a giant
flowering water lily
like the accidental collision
of a coffee table and a parasol
in a goldfish bowl
amid the pan-pipe music
unripe bananas make
while outside the glass
some fur coats slithered past
under the iced-up botanist statue
stuck in siberia at twenty below
and joni sang on my ipod
I wish there was a river
I could skate away on

there was a sofa too
and a rustling of refugee birds
or maybe something bigger
before steps came down
the spiral staircase
above a patch of colour
I hadn't noticed before
and I thought as I waited
to greet the old painter
o coleridge o de quincey o
all you head in the clouds romantics
no-one mentioned that about opium
such a long finish
such o value for money

§

penny lane

she finds this being
angry with him
makes it easier

she wants someone else
she needs the story
to make it easier

she picks and rubs
at her anger
she's afraid too

she might be
leaving home
she may have left

she's a locked room
mystery he's shut outside
with all their records

clicks and jumps
one by one
they can't be played

§

william brown street

the mood's interrogative
the future's monochrome
and we don't like
your chances much pal

when did you last
see your father
a question we should all
ask ourselves
from time to time

the answer
though
that stretches out
in all directions

§

hope street

that band of ours
we never made it
came too late
weren't that good
didn't want it quite
enough so off we went
on our separate tracks

one was last seen
busking and giving it
the alehouse strum
further up the coast
his teeth undimmed
his dreams unguessable

one found his
serious work face
left in a boat and got
heavier round the heart

dreams not wanted
on voyage

and the third getting
older but not answering
the door to time passing
finally bought himself
the guitar of his dreams
just before the morning
his fingers didn't work

but old friends
it's not position hopeless
it's situation excellent
to make the comeback from
elsewhere or thereabouts
retune to vestapol
dig out the bottleneck
de-coke the gob-iron
and see what happens

what happens after
so many more years
with the teach-yourself book
of those holy grail
bound to fail
less than fab
midlife drab
twelve bar mode
further on down the road

blues

§

abbey road

I have to ask
who was that
in the photo

if that's who
I have to say
he's not here now

I took the same
zebra crossing
but none of it
is what it was
poor lad poor lad
like all of us

§

red square

on the long and winding
road of restaurants
well north of moscow
the group at the next table
the ones with kalashnikovs
were only actors
fortunately

beatles fans too
they were singing along
to the house band's
stately take on yesterday

and plonking michelle
without the french bit
though no-one put in
requests for revolution
or back in the ussr
just in case

some beers later
I pointed to their toys and said
so happiness is a warm gun
and they roared and toasted me
before our translator asked
did I get it right
aly did you say
happiness is a warm
to be polite vagina

I said yulia right there
that's rock and roll
so here's to glasnost
and weapons of choice

with these understandings
firmly in place
next year
mccartney played red square

Famous Russian Poet

A winter afternoon, Western Siberia. Low wattage and a murmuration of librarians. Serious guests from foreign parts lost between translation and digestion. She stands, one woman with her pile of cataloguing, and later she'll write in her secret diary: what came over me and what was I expecting? Good afternoon, she says, I am famous Russian poet. That night a visitor will write in his journal: in Russia even the librarians are poets. What does that say about the Russian soul? What does that explain about the state of their libraries?

Next day she's detailed to herd the visitors down the spine of a glistening pavement. To the left, the buildings' cascade of melting ice and stucco. To the right, grey-brown dinosaur wakes of trolley-buses. That night a visitor will write in his journal: this is a country where even keeping to the straight and narrow gets you wet from both sides. That night she'll begin her poetic sequence: Welcome to Russia. No, a line through that. Famous Russian Poet. Better. Maybe. Why not?

Continuity

1
Steel doors
make good stairwells
make good neighbours.

The archive of loose tongues
they threw open
downtown only yesterday
has a new lock.

Mother says:
all these years
whispering
and now
we're whispering again.

2
Yet it will be written.
It will, even like this.

The pencil stub.
The birchbark book.

This museum case says
done and dusted now,
our prison-camp years.

But maybe—

buy a pencil
on the way out?

3
The name of this building
was State Security.

Who's in there now?
We don't know.
It's a secret.

Footprints in the snow
go in and out
and you might have
the impression:
fewer coming out.

And you might count
just to be sure.
But better not.
Being a secret.

Navigation by statue

Best seen from the north,
the leader in gunmetal;
still wanting more from us,
still pointing somewhere gone
through snow and smoke and leaves.
And by the way, we're
always grateful for the leaves.

The eastern approach
at the corner of his eye,
that's dead zone, blindside
you wouldn't want to count on,
stealing back through the blizzard
brushing off black market smuts.

Westward, large classes gather
to count the icicles along
that long-extended arm.
You know his methods, children.
Each of you will be wrong
but all part of today's
correct answer, which is 5.571.

On the south side, edging
inside the sheltering static
of cosmonaut and eternal flame,
we can speak our minds
quite quietly and not too near
the craning flowerbeds,
we can swap tales behind
his back to smuggle

across our various borders.
Yes, we know he's dead
but old habits die last.
As we once said about hope.

The odd splash of colour

Blue

She gave me
her bunch of meadow flowers.
Her mother said:
for the colour of your eyes.

It's true.
I looked in the mirror.
A caged blue,
still hungry for sky.

Green

Dipping bread in egg
while the dacha melted,
I was aware of a poem
shuffling its feet by the door
but got distracted as usual
by the new packs of heritage seeds.

By the time I came back
from the vegetable patch,
sorry to say that the poem
had changed its mind
and soon enough followed
the usual local autumn with
our usual hand-me-downs:
tomatoes picked and stored still green.

Black

What she brought to the table:
candlelight and fearless jokes;
a bottle cool from the kiosk;
all the flowers of someone else's season;
silver flickers on a warm throat.

All he brought was black,
although at the time
it helped everything shine.
It was a complicated darkness
but one he knew his way around in.
Which came in useful, later on.

Red

Overnight the fishermen
lost their hermitages
out on the ice; one more thing
they'll be thoughtful about
as they cast and reel
among the summer flies,
yearning for the crackling skin
they'll walk in winter.

Women meantime brought in meat
from exile on the frozen balconies
and found some a bit spoiled.
Yes, we still know these moments.

And you, little red boat, marooned
above the storm-channel, castaway
of last year's floods, soul-mate,

you felt the tug again and floated.
Went spinning. Filled with water.

Gold

She helped them
hide the icons
and got old, waiting.

White covered golden autumn.
Wind-spun snow.
A comb of birch.

After each spring of the air,
a spring of the ground.
Amnesty for snowdrops,
meltwater underfoot and
other wonders, just enough
to be going on with.

Another fairy tale

I'm that part of the forest
where there aren't any
soft leaves to fall
and here to the nearest souls
is a long day's sift of needles.

But you can rest here,
dear, in my moss-cottage
under its roof of green light
where dusk soon gets its way
and only this basket lies
between us and our bedtime stories.
Choose, taste a mushroom from it;
I promise I picked them
only upwind of the accident.

One will turn you
to a little yellow bird
that zigzags like a needle
to the astonishing treetops
and forgets everything
but dawn and horizons.

One will change you
to a brown dog, waking
uneasy in the early light,
soon off to find the dappled scent
of yesterday and remember
only where it comes from.

The third will certify you
hero of the wildwood

as you'll need to be
to stay with me forever.
I say nothing, I can do nothing
but watch you, knowing
which choice no-one ever tasted,
watch without much hope as
your hand hesitates. Hesitates.

Exiles

1
There was my father's
old mouth-organ
but on the way
he dropped it.

There's still a song.
He said
it wasn't always
about twilight.

2
Twilight, daylight or
the hours unlit,
no-one else heard
the sea-birds calling.
But he'd tune into his
gull-stations just to drown
the big noise hereabouts,
our heroic river chugging dull
saltless marches to the horizon.

He warned me not
to settle for fresh water.
Bring your own seagulls:
those were often his
last words on the matter.

3
I said:
I have no seagulls.
He said:
I'll leave you mine.

But really all I got
was that song
in its veil of dusk
and static on the gull-radio.

Laying my flowers down,
I'd like to say
I'm listening, though.
Still listening.

Recall

It was a time of victory parades,
or a time of psychiatric wards,
or you can try for zero recollection
but still you'll get what you're given.

These moments that didn't make
the shelter of the diaries,
not all froze to death and
some would say: unfortunately.

When (just like one of our old gods)
I purged you from my photographs,
what I gained where you'd posed
was a shapelier tree-trunk,
more fragrant beds of hyacinth,
a sliver extra of the grey dam
that holds back murky waters.

But you—serial revenant,
my blurred commissar
of the abandoned plan—
here's your false smile coming
through, coming through again
and snapshot after snapshot
haunted from the shutter-click
by this ectoplasm, heartache.

Edge

So love let go
its hold and fell forever:
vertigo,
a surge of cold,
like the dead I'd leant above.

And these days
I'm drawn to anything
like steps cut in a rock face,
parapets and ledges
and the ground
beyond the guard rail,

all the windswept edges,
all the jagged endings
of where we think we live.

Lenin Street

Babushkas are cascading boots first
down the glassy floes along Lenin,
padded like seal pups but not so wide-eyed.
Old school, hard school to the end,
they learned the lesson early; get up
fast before the judges mark you down,
before you have to register as fallen.

Except for one, who kept the faith
with concrete steps that weren't there again
today; who needs a rescue party
to prise and heave her from the iron
stomp of gravity, replant her in these times
of no-one's job, no-one's responsibility.
Not speaking out in haste, that was engrained
too, but she unpacks her semaphore kit
of shrugs and head-shakes and hand-sweeps
and this is her state-of-the-nation:

In our old Siberia, at least we knew
how to deal with snow. Whose fault it was
when things went wrong. What to do about that.

Magic abroad

Here come the Westerners,
from their enchanted lands
of tulips in December:
a bumpy transit of democracy,
a slightly creased symposium
on heavier-than-air flight,
packed like exotic fruit
in one of our historic planes.

They're coming down to land
in a trademark blizzard, discussing
with diversionary earnestness
the meaning of sky hieroglyphs,
snowflake symmetries, the whole
dazzling crystal library of infinity.
They know enough to know
you never land in the same
snowstorm twice. Sometimes,
they also know, not even once.

Here's an internal drum-roll
for the height they're losing so
lumpily, breath held for the moment
when the clouds go solid.
The clouds go solid and the plane
taxis on them, furry with whiteness.
A good trick—they could watch it
over and over. Stairs glide
towards them, a bus, a terminal.

The legerdemain of the passport!
The lovely immigration officer,

cupid's bow mouth pursed, tools
of her scepticism at the ready
(light, magnifying glass), still
can't see how it's done.
Her smile is her baffled applause.

Not every suitcase can be Houdini,
though there are usually some escapes.
Sympathetic hands stretch towards
the carousel's failures, padlocked,
strapped and chrysalid with tape.

And they're out, to where Lyuba
waits with her driver. She's rehearsed
the foreign language spell for greeting,
he's fine-tuned his spattered Lada.
He likes this weather. Siberia works.
His tools are blowtorch and baseball bat.

Thirty degrees below freezing,
vodka flows thick and oily.
Tentative air-kisses speak of a changed
world, smoke without fire. They'll see.
The car skims the potholes, on ice
that's maybe thicker than it looks.

In Arcadia

...and fleet the time carelessly, as they did in the golden world.
William Shakespeare: *As you like it*

Thy necessity is greater than mine.
Sir Philip Sidney: attributed last words

metamorphoses (i)

recall how rocks
how shouting grinding
cruel winds and
disdain of salt water
and

then the air
blew silk and gold
to wake me
in the shore waves
still in life

and all day resting
by the sea
where adventures
wash and change
there read
storm wrack of
almost letters
with such a
lightning of beauty

a heavy charge
as lit
my road out
my new calling
to cut the thread
the harmony of
green thoughts
break out

words and
have come to your ears
yes even to those
most settled estates
strange tragedies

my tongue adventure
call it metamorphosis
and shipwreck
and princess ruin and
the slow fade
of shepherds

into arcadia
then

§

metamorphoses (ii)

welcome
he bowed low
to arcadia

endless
charmed circle
heavenly
hellish
maze of longing
dungeon state of
the captived will
and so forth

but pity for your

poor mouth
too parched for
the one true question
of a gentleman abroad
which is to say
what raiment is best
for such weather
as these days
which is to say
who are you
to be
here
sir

the answer
I judge lying
not in deceptive
humble weeds
of the weave
called ancient shepherd
nor the princely range
of royal entitlement
in silks and armour

instead
let me commend
the cypress pattern
dark tufts across
a profound black
much in demand
since death will always
change the tale
and is the tale and
we name this one
dress graves

for which
many an eye
will moisten
many a door will open
in arcadia

§

exequies (i)

a door opened
that one
worn oak

depth of night
over a wax-candle
when the weather is
sorrow

cold was
drawing the curtain
the breath
stopped
and whatever words
too late

last of her
red flakes in the element
and once out
never such black

§

shepherds (i)

armed men
and great ones
beyond question
favoured us
all the little square
with these words
though brief

mourn boldly
blackness will shine
cries will be music
a temple of
woeful language
waits your pleasure

into a time
of such trembling
courtesy
you that way

we this
with regretfully
the best of
careless
shepherd youth
to stitch up
war matters

§

princesses (i)

lights
there will be lights
before the sun comes
there will be
sounds and stir

a little clearing
of the mind
the woods
cross-hatched
with policy

hawk
hound
horse
have the smell of it

princess
blood royal
have they told you
all the nets are
here for you

§

exequies (ii)

their faces
a great number of torches
death
shined through the mist

the wound
hurt
like a rose
he heard
the sun fall

not yet
not yet

§

princesses (ii)

she lay
a moonlit
altar
blotted
marks of
soft hand
all her fair length

she
hid her face
and that was
a whispering note
a cloud passing

then
o you stars

§

metamorphoses (iii)

driven
to the river's side
running
winding
till held by
banks of loving earth
she felt
the sun's darts
o coldness
then a different
sun

cypress
bowing her
green locks
she stood
beyond pain of
hunted
in a grace
disdaining
his force
his purpose

the god
ran past

§

shepherds (ii)

what made him
so pine
it was beautiful
indifference
the sky by night
and the sea

what made her
sigh
his voice and
love songs till
she thought
a wolf at sheep

and
long for
his turning
away
on the night track

that left to her
dark sea

a breathing

§

exequies (iii)

lay
blood pendant
darkening

but beautiful
still as sleep
as the lake
not ruffled

this before
sun and dogs
remembered
their appetites

the day was
time was

they remembered

§

shepherds (iii)

he said
not a sheep
have I
or had ever
none the less
my essence and
calling is
shepherd

said I
when I close
my eyes
I am
the blind king of paphlagonia

so was born
in an afternoon
arcadian
philosophy

§

princesses (iii)

leaves
how the leaves
descended
and if there were
somewhere near
as she believed
a secret arbour
it was beyond
her compass
racked with jealousy

bewitched
thralldom
she felt
the very words
an unmeasurable sting

it was in
a great wood
where she found
her voice for
courage
and sang
love
you make the planet
dark

leaves fell
and love sang back
o lady
welcome to
your late solitary life

§

metamorphoses (iv)

after some
months found
in a little wood
her shady hanging
as it were forgotten

a careless
nature had set
feather
glitter
upon her body

consider
the small foot
velvet and skin and
like a garment
open to show
the truer

hair gold wire
breastplate
persistence
of the device
never more valiant

to mark where she
beyond eyes
by a door
opened in the green

was gone

§

shepherds (iv)

he played
a rustic pipe

the dogs lay
charmed
to drowsing

wild natures
moved in
closer
he felt himself
not shepherd but
a god
of those mountains

the sheep
though
they knew
astray
when they heard it

§

princesses (iv)

the sky
overclouded

a quaking
a paleness

think
the cold ashes of
princesses
lips
in forever
denial

think
the unperformed
musics
the undinted
silences

then at last
rain's
lamenting
at the door
and vain to knock
and vain to knock

§

metamorphoses (v)

old men
shook their weeds

and sighed
dolefully
most dolefully
the question being
poetry
what had it
come to
in arcadia

swan and
lute
measures
mistaken
by the panting heart
in those little books
of four or five leaves

a coastline
wreckage
not soon enough
swept
from our marble
atlas

evenings
at the bashful
theatre
presenting
shepherds in
red face

smoke
from a green fire
in the tomb
margins

blown
here and there
and no such place

shook their weeds
the old men
sighed like
old men will
does that
answer your question
stranger

§

exequies (iv)

so
his fame
engraved
in marble and
lamenting
into
bless his eyes
that huge
loneliness
across the strait
he passed
dumb

love was
retired and
elsewhere
the mountain
where it had been

moss
as ever
on the move

he also
would be forgotten
in arcadia

§

metamorphoses (vi)

I cast aside
the cypress weeds
I trod a measure
with shepherds
I danced the
labyrinth
of leaves
and roots
I drank deep
crimson
from the goatskins

woke to hear
seabirds cry
and the waves
and felt breath
of wood
move under me

so closed my eyes
so woke again to
a port with

its sea-names
with its
name for me
a welcome home
and salt tears
questions

answered only
friends

I was in
arcadia

Lightning Source UK Ltd.
Milton Keynes UK
UKOW03f0630140314

228137UK00001B/99/P